IN THE YEAR OF OUR MAKING & UNMAKING

ISBN: 978-1-7363695-1-7

Cover art & design by Fraver | www.fraver.com
Book design by Chelsea D'Errico - Frontier Poetry

Frederick Speers
Visit my website at www.frederickspeers.com

Published in the United States of America by Frontier Poetry

www.frontierpoetry.com

PRAISE FOR *IN THE YEAR OF OUR MAKING & UNMAKING*

"A spartan prosody resembling the brief notations on a calendar forms the foundation of this suite of poems composed inside enormous silences: flowers isolated in fields, the bare spots around them saying so much about living, thriving, surviving: 'knowing/ better—// & yet,/ every day,// daring to/ step outside'." –**D. A. Powell**

"Written in a series of cells that are reminiscent of the cells of days, and the larger field of the month as time amounts across a cycle of reckoning, the poems *In The Year of Our Making & Unmaking* are subtly evocative of space, and movement, specifically of the archaic notion of rhythm that is not a regular measure or dance, but rather improvised, and provisional shapes we're able to compose out of and against the overall (and overwhelming) flow of bodies in the world. The visual prosody of the poems opens up our reading through this elsewhere rhythm: 'On some / plateau // in the / distance // the universe // is a flower,' is not exactly a gesture the poem literally holds if we're playing by the rules, reading left to right, top to bottom; it is, however, one of many such constellations, epiphanies of language & image that this book makes possible for the reader to alight upon and experience as a momentary freedom, a heaven in a wild flower." –**Jeffrey Pethybridge**

"Friends, read this slim wonder of a book. Urgent, moving, and restlessly inventive, *In the Year of Our Making & Unmaking* is both an accounting of and reckoning with mortality, beauty, and love. Frederick Speers constructs a physical body for time itself—a body that breathes, breaks, thrives, and passes right before our eyes in the shapes the poems make on the page. Elegies, love songs, and pastorals find new incarnations in Speers' hands. This is a book to brand our hearts, dazzle our minds, and refresh our sense of what a poem can be." –**Kirun Kapur**

"Even more resonant upon a year of immutable losses, *In the Year of Our Making & Unmaking* is a meditation on the limits of the human body: the distance between us—void of human contact, in a field of buildings—where only the sea is heard 'echoing the sky.' It is in the natural world that we find solace, in the company of 'the wildflowers/ with their different, if somewhat repetitive play/ up & down the quiet median.' Another day in quarantine, now made clearer by the absence of human interaction, where the memory of each other makes the next moment possible. Speers perceives a world that is dark yet made meaningful through memory." –**Ruben Quesada**

"Speers' poems take place in a time that's circular and layered, offering us 'old and new ways of being.' Months are blue, receptive, spilling one into the next, thin skinned. Months may make promises that outline failure, or refuse to play the field, or visit old haunts. Hours chart everything from moral failings to a Black-capped chickadee at the bird-feeder. Moving deftly from fear and sorrow to vast, blooming hope, Speers makes music and sense of an inimitable version of our world, one we are making even as it makes us. One 'making me feel/ like all you've/ made in the field,/ a flower feeling I've made.' This collection is wild with life." –**Rachel DeWoskin**

An irremediably unhappy person is outside the laws of the earth. Any connection between him and society is severed finally. And since, sooner or later, every individual is doomed to irremediable unhappiness, the last word of philosophy is loneliness. —Lev Shestov

When there's no future
How can there be sin
We're the flowers in the dustbin
—Sex Pistols

Blue Month

<table>
<tr><td>the day of
your death</td><td>any day
in my life</td><td>is
a frame</td><td>for</td><td>what
is</td><td>& isn't</td><td>impossible
to lose,</td></tr>
<tr><td>an aura</td><td>around</td><td>the space</td><td>where
the leaf</td><td>was,</td><td>is
becoming</td><td>clearer,</td></tr>
<tr><td>unfairly
blue,</td><td>the likes</td><td>of which I,</td><td>in truth,</td><td>never</td><td>thought</td><td>to touch,</td></tr>
<tr><td>having
radiated</td><td>of</td><td>nothing
that much</td><td>myself,</td><td>&
now</td><td>that it is</td><td>later, far
later,</td></tr>
<tr><td>breathless
you,</td><td>you</td><td>hum me
this tune</td><td></td><td></td><td></td><td></td></tr>
</table>

One Month Spilling Over into the Next

<table>
<tr><td></td><td></td><td></td><td>if the
universe</td><td>is</td><td>a field,
& you</td><td>are there
walking</td></tr>
<tr><td>toward me</td><td>on some
plateau</td><td>in the
distance</td><td>extending</td><td>itself,
in fact</td><td>extending
all</td><td>in all the
ways</td></tr>
<tr><td>that matter, if</td><td>the universe</td><td>is a flower,</td><td>tell me</td><td>the first</td><td>you see, &</td><td>likewise I</td></tr>
<tr><td>in good faith</td><td>will say what
I find;</td><td>then</td><td>let's
compare</td><td>roots,
stems</td><td>leaves,
blooms:</td><td>if from the
same</td></tr>
<tr><td>family,
consider</td><td>each, slight
difference:</td><td>red,
maroon</td><td>petal,
wound—</td><td></td><td></td><td></td></tr>
</table>

Receptive Month

				—& if they are	from different	families
how might	they be similar:	blue	maybe, blue	as blue	as the sea	echoing
the sky:	one generation	of Blues	singers	showing up	in the performance	of the next
like cloud- bursts,	drum rolls,	our lives	emptied throughout	our lives	filling in for each other	old & new
ways of being	not the same	empty pool	likening this	to that, a reflection	like nothing else	on earth

Rupture Month in the Logic of Remembering

<table>
<tr><td>you—you make</td><td>me</td><td>feel</td><td>like a flower</td><td>in a field</td><td>all</td><td>alone</td></tr>
<tr><td>you make me</td><td>alone,</td><td>feeling</td><td>like</td><td>a flower</td><td>making</td><td>a field</td></tr>
<tr><td>of feelings</td><td>without</td><td>you,</td><td>making me</td><td>feel</td><td>like all</td><td>you’ve made</td></tr>
<tr><td>in the field,</td><td>a flower</td><td>feeling</td><td>I’ve made</td><td>your making</td><td>a field</td><td>of me, alone,</td></tr>
<tr><td>you make me,</td><td></td><td></td><td></td><td></td><td></td><td></td></tr>
<tr><td></td><td>feel—</td><td></td><td></td><td></td><td></td><td></td></tr>
</table>

Month of the Anonymous North American

		god of	sod,	carpet	each	bald spot
with Bluegrass	the forgotten leaves of	St. Augustine	bent like	weary	Buffalo	among Wheatgrass
a thorough mixture	past & future	whispering	in bed as though	memory	wandering quietly	lasting in the shapes
of this moment	stirring	the multitude	asleep	deep & fertile	alarms	of this life
held in my arms	what is never just	uniform	or a little	yielding		

Month with Tripod & Shrine

					when I converted	when I was cured
(one hasn't	happened yet)	though I see them	next to each other	all the time,	gorgeous men	amusing to a point,
something that feels	in- between	there	&—	not there	moaning with	silence
to find	happiness & sorrow	fucking	forever	in the back room,	hands on my head	calling my name
in the dark	of my bones,	another's light	taking root—	becoming	my charge,	my only charge

In the Hour of My Moral Failings

Its wings flutter, what I thought   was a sprig
of Queen-Ann's-Lace: one idea   making
clear it's another: the butterfly   flies
from view. For many, to disconnect   is
a privilege, like tuning out   the news.
Like the painter, who dabbled   in oils, once telling me
that to make a scene
even sadder, just add a point   of light.
True, I will not think of you today —   all
day & with dwindling   sadness:
every gutter & storm-drain leads
away. At any rate, I'm still   here,
watching the wildflowers   in front of me,
with their different,   if
somewhat repetitive, play
up & down the quiet median—   I
can't shake this feeling
I'm their dark audience   today.

Month of Promises Outlining the Failure

I don't believe	I doubt as much as	I did;	somewhat unnatural,	given time	& today's	god- forsaken
 scenes—	praying half- heartedly	as they do;	now I find	faith in my life	beginning a second	 skin, soon
enough & shedding just	enough to allow	a good boy	in a bad lot	to fall	behind what	he could have been,
sluffed in rings,	the transparent cost to being	always in need,	begging for what	have you—	evolution's love?—	like an itch
for what can never be	found— even when	it draws blood				

Thin-Skinned Month

			you	sick	fuck, is this	what gets you
off? The sheer	mass	of our	collective	loss? To think,	you	don’t exist in the slightest,
at least not	in the way	one might	picture	you—& still	you	get
our sweet music	&	the final word	about the music	we’ve composed	for you— in fact	you get both
the notes & the	strummed silences	that, as we wake,	without	fail echo		

Month Refusing to Play the Field

					here, the center of all	these movements,
somehow remains	unmoved—	honey- comb,	honey	—if love is	Good & always	Good, then
love I'm afraid	love can't be in search of	what	is Good:	the core belief	not withstanding	the rest
dance where	the love-	that- dares-	not-	speak-	its-name	&
the-death-	my-kin-	will-not- claim	encircle worlds	so sickly sweet	night & day—	come, follow me

The Hour of Death's Herald as this Black-Capped Chickadee at the Bird-Feeder in Our Backyard

Endearing,
isn't it, how
your little song
clearly ends
as you eat,
each note turning
into its own
unbecoming
seed-shell,
seed-shell,
seed-shell?

Month for the Rest of My Life

pill + pill	pill + pill	pill + pill	pill + pill	pill + pill	pill + pill	pill + pill
pill + pill	pill + pill	pill	pill + pill	pill + pill	pill + pill	pill + pill
pill + pill	pill + pill	pill + pill	pill + pill	pill + pill	pill + pill	pill + pill
pill + pill	pill + pill	pill + pill	pill + pill	pill + pill	pill + pill	pill + pill
pill + pill	pill + pill	pill + pill				

Exposed Month with Red & Yellow

			every living gay	kid has been called	*faggot*!	from across
the empty lot,	walking somewhere	alone—	as all the various	lots, everywhere	forge like candle wax	to form
this single flame—	smoking the twisted rope	we burn without	change,	revealing so much more	by hiding it,	flaunting it, or
walking somewhere	all the same;	knowing better—	& yet, every day,	daring to step outside	. . . clearly	there can be
no such thing	as divine love	without us	burning bound- lessly	the cold here & there		

Hour of Paths, Steps & Lanterns

Cloud after cloud after cloud—the night
that night wouldn't be anything momentous, I could
tell: grass on the grave-plots all trimmed
—except the last on the hill, where the gray overlooks.
Wouldn't be
anything
noteworthy
I could tell already
from here, nothing at all so neat
about that lonely headstone—only that it leaned a bit, was
soot-colored & cool against the disheveled crest of the hill
—but mostly, one would say, overlooked. Soon

where flowers had once been placed, nearer to where I
stood, something like petals grew, as it started to drizzle;
then another, a little fainter & then another, further up—O, if
followed, I figured, this might be new.
I knelt down
on the wet
path hoping for
a closer look.
(There was no moon.) I did, then, only what I felt
you would do. Before dawn, up the same weathered stairs
I wandered ahead of myself, step
after step after step—humming a minor tune.

Month Revisiting Old Haunts

<table>
<tr><td></td><td></td><td></td><td></td><td></td><td>if it's
true</td><td>I won't
survive</td></tr>
<tr><td>my
inflammation,</td><td>this
phoenix</td><td>of in-
difference;</td><td>if it is to
mean</td><td>anything in
the thrilling</td><td>dark, it
must be,</td><td>my
friends,</td></tr>
<tr><td>that this
desire,</td><td>unloosed,
will be</td><td>you,
you with</td><td>every last
gray</td><td>& resplendent
feather</td><td>of you,</td><td>you,</td></tr>
<tr><td>you,</td><td>you</td><td>shaking</td><td>prophecy,</td><td>if you wish,
out</td><td>from you</td><td>taking the
stem</td></tr>
<tr><td>of my un-
petaled hope</td><td>for your</td><td>own, then
leaving it</td><td>all behind
for</td><td>others to lift
up, high</td><td>enough
& freely</td><td>in time</td></tr>
</table>

www.ingramcontent.com/pod-product-compliance
Ingram Content Group UK Ltd.
Pitfield, Milton Keynes, MK11 3LW, UK
UKHW051333070726
13610UKWH00015B/97